Guy Wires

Elisavietta Ritchie

Books and Chapbooks by Elisavietta Ritchie

IN HASTE I WRITE YOU THIS NOTE: STORIES & HALF-STORIES (e-book, 2015)

TIGER UPSTAIRS ON CONNECTICUT AVENUE (2013)

FEATHERS, OR, LOVE ON THE WING (with artists Megan Richard, Suzanne Shelden, 2013)

FROM THE ARTIST'S DEATHBED (chapbook 2012)

CORMORANT BEYOND THE COMPOST (2011)

REAL TOADS (chapbook, 2008)

AWAITING PERMISSION TO LAND (2006)

THE SPIRIT OF THE WALRUS (chapbook 2005)

IN HASTE I WRITE YOU THIS NOTE: STORIES & HALF-STORIES, (2000)

THE ARC OF THE STORM (1998)

ELEGY FOR THE OTHER WOMAN: NEW & SELECTED POEMS (1996)

WILD GARLIC: THE JOURNAL OF MARIA X. (novella in verse, chapbook 1995}

A WOUND-UP CAT AND OTHER BEDTIME STORIES (chapbook, 1993)

FLYING TIME: STORIES & HALF-STORIES (1986, 1988)

THE PROBLEM WITH EDEN (chapbook 1985)

RAKING THE SNOW (1982)

A SHEATH OF DREAMS AND OTHER GAMES (chapbook, 1976)

TIGHTENING THE CIRCLE OVER EEL COUNTRY (1974)

TIMBOT (novella-in-verse, chapbook, 1970)

Poetry Anthologies Created:

THE DOLPHIN'S ARC: Poems on Endangered Creatures of the Sea (1986)

FINDING THE NAME (1983)

Guy Wires

Elisavietta Ritchie

Elisavietta Ritchie

Poets' Choice Publishing

Copyright © 2015 Poets' Choice Publishing

Introduction © 2015 Richard Harteis

Printed in the United States of America

Editor: Richard Harteis

Book and cover design by Suzanne Shelden, (sheldenstudios.com)

Cover art and photography by Suzanne Shelden (sheldenstudios.com)

Consultant work:
www.WilliamMeredithFoundation.org

Bulk discounts available through
www.poets-choice.com

Library of Congress Control Number: 2015936713

ISBN 978-0-9909257-2-9

Poets' Choice Publishing
337 Kitemaug Road
Uncasville, Ct. 06382

Poets-Choice.com

Acknowledgments

The author thanks the editors of several journals which published these poems, many in earlier versions, and for their personal encouragement:

"Adolphe Blondheim: *The Decoration:*" *Loch Raven Review,* 2014;

"A Gift of Tomatoes:" *The Ledge,* 2014; *Garden Blessings,* June Cotner, editor, 2014; translated into Korean for anthology;

"Au Chateau de Chillon:" *Ann Arbor Review,* vol. 14, 2015;

"Cecelia in the Parking Lot at Dawn:" *Reckless Writing Poetry Anthology,* Chatterhouse Press, 2014;

"Cecelia's New Life Rag:" *Canto,* circa 1986;

"Cecelia Was Born in Chicago And This Imprinted on Her Life:" *Beltway Poetry Journal,* prosepoem issue, 2013;

"Confronting the Mountain in Tbilisi:" *Ann Arbor Review,* vol. 14, 2015;

"Crabbing in January?" *Reckless Writing Poetry Anthology,* Chatterhouse Press, 2014;

"The Famous Poet Limps to the Stage with Her Cane:" *The Broadkill Review,* 2014;

"Feline:" *Ann Arbor Review,* vol. 14, 2015;

"Guy Wires:" *Northern Liberties Review,* 2014;

"Heidegger at the Breakfast Table:" *Blue Unicorn,* 2002; semi-finalist *Emily Dickinson Award Anthology* Universities West Press, Glenn Reed, editor, 2002;

"The Potentially Unfulfilled Crimson Hen:" *End of 83,* 2014;

"Preliminary Experiments:" *End of 83,* 2014;

"Photograph in Black and White:" *Lalitamba,* 2015;

"Quick-Change Artists:" *End of 83,* 2014;

"Searching Hong Kong for Chocolate:" *Journeys Along the Silk Road,* Harry Yang editor, Lost Tower Publications, 2015;

"Trying to Tell a Blind Man about the Moon's Eclipse:" *Ann Arbor Review,* vol. 14, 2015;

"Those Old Blueberries:" *Visions International,* 2015;

"You Invite Me to Visit Your Coliseum:" *Lalitamba,* 2015;

"Visitations: Two Vultures:" *Potomac Review, 2014;*

"Visiting Hours:" *Visions International,* 2015.

Fragments of poems on the section dividers are from the author's mini-chapbook *A Tangle of Spiders, 2008, The Canadian Writers' Journal* and *Blue Unicorn,* in which some of the individual poems had first appeared, and in the author's books *Awaiting Permission to Land* and *The Arc of the Storm.*

Particular thanks to Clyde Henri Farnsworth, Carol Jennings, Philip Kurata, Elisabeth Stevens, Myra Sklarew, Susan Sonde and Martin Tucker for advice on individual poems, and above all to Richard Harteis and Suzanne Shelden for creating the whole book.

dedicated
to poets and writers around the world
who have suffered under oppressive regimes
and to those who will

Introduction

When one reads the exquisite short title poem of GUY WIRES, the temptation, of course is to assign Elisavietta Ritchie the moniker of Spider Woman. And how wonderful and potent that the stuff of which she spins her web is love. This is a very serious poet, who weaves her poems with the tensile strength of spider silk, greater than the same weight of steel, and with much greater elasticity.

Her poems make remarkable connections between her manic intelligence and the dear particulars of the world. Line by line, she pulls us forward into her creation, and we lie there, calm, mesmerized and grateful for the new take on the world she invariably wraps us in. There is a lot of talk these days of the "wise woman," something like Erda in Wagner's *Ring Cycle*, that makes a reader realize they are in the presence of a mind worth hearing. "Your dog knows./She's different when/the moon is full," she tells us.

But the poems swing through the human passions of sex, politics, and other worldly appetites with the agility of a Peter Parker on a joyful romp through the canyons of Manhattan. She has thrown a pentagram web over her private world, organizing a lifetime of experience and joy into five architectural sections - one thinks of Frost's notion that the final poem in a book of poetry is the book's organization.

AT THE EDGE salutes dissident poets she has known and supported in a long life of taking responsibility for her actions: "Yet, in this land/ a poem can... land you in jail," and, "I have told others 'write with your blood.'" In *Sisterhood: Mothers of Prisoners,* she commiserates with the Russian poet Anna Akhmatova, "May we at least find/ uncertain solace in our sisterhood." This is a beautifully felt group of poems, told with beautiful simplicity and power:

> How can shapes and blots
> of lives steaming with pain
> and so much love be forgot.

The poems in WEAVERS become an *ars poetica* for the poet, and often reflect on the great mystery of death.

In time I'll go blind
so while the lunatic moon
crowns from the sea
must write fast
snatch at stars –

In part three, EXPLORATIONS, Ritchie alerts us to the fact that she is coloring outside the lines. *The Thing about Drinking*, for example treats us to multiple personalities "in a single bound," as it were. Some of these poems are simply a riot. After a long plodding trek to find a beach and finally have a swim, she is greeted with a signboard reading:

BEWARE! RIPTIDES! RISKY! BOXJELLYFISH LETHAL! SHARKS! CROCODILES!

The last two sections of GUY WIRES imagine other lives in the animal kingdom: FELLOWS; and, celebrate the moving force, love, pushing all of creation forward in the final section of the web titled CENTRAL. We leave them to you, no comment, to peruse at your pleasure, but only to say how proud and pleased we are to have been bitten by this exotic, startling, and powerful creature. What a poet!

Richard Harteis, Editor
Poets' Choice Publishing
Kensington, Md. 3/20/2015

Table of Contents

I AT THE EDGE

II WEAVERS

III EXPLORATIONS

IV FELLOWS

V CENTRAL

I   AT THE EDGE

Bless the spider
who spins guy wires
          across corners,
                    webs connect edges

Guy Wires

for a foreign writer, visiting

You sat yesterday on my balcony.
Untrimmed, the magnolia's leaves
wreathed your head, and a bee
examined your words as if visas.

I served you melons and wine,
you spoke of mangoes and palms,
a child throwing stones at a plane,
of pear-tree roots gripping a tomb.

You've flown across half the earth,
explored and lectured, praised, criticized
as instructed before you set forth.
We told our stories, kissed and cried.

Alone, still breathless this morning,
I note a spider skein the cat ignores
in the slant of sun, guyed from this worn
wrought-iron chair to your chair.

Elisavietta Ritchie

Trying to Tell a Blind Man
About the Moon's Eclipse

Your dog knows.
She's different when
the moon is full:

her black-and-tawny fur stands up,
she crouches, claws, breaks through
screen doors, zigzags up the hill—

moon madness still
allowed for dogs.
Tonight coyotes howl.

So even with no calendar
in Braille, you're alerted
something's up…

The full moon crowns.
Soon the earth will throw
a bloody shadow—

I will describe it only later
to spare you my excitement.
You have sensed it anyway.

I guide you to our usual meadow,
we talk of weather, opera, birds,
and did I forget to buy dog food?

All the time I know you are
greedy for sights you cannot see,
feelings you ought not have.

A Gift of Tomatoes

You bring me the tight bloody suns of October
snatched from vines entangled, untied, hiding
green snakes and black-and-gold spiders.

They escape from a basket of wicker,
through your fingers, from your hands,
harvest moons crowning through hills—

They roll, swell, burst in my palms,
bleed into fate's crevasses,
redden our destiny's map.

I try to tame them under my knife
with sugar and parsley and salt.
Their blood burns the cuts in my hands.

Their flesh lights my throat with their glow
all winter I dream of gardens, pungent, cold,
where tomatoes loll, still green and hard,

among furry spiders and shimmering snakes
till the carmine moon bursts through the sky—

Photograph in Black and White

Oaks hunch black
above the farmhouse white
we borrowed last night

The black door locks
night's warmth inside
our stolen night

You stand beside
gray hollyhocks
beyond gray lawn

your striped shirt wrinkles gray
eyelids wrinkle gray
gray fists clench tight

before your homeward flight
to that dark land
where only snow is white

Gray lips unsmiling clamp
in all you must not speak
I must not write

      Or write with wax on a handkerchief
      fashion a frame to contain
      all that grief

      Words beneath the wax
      in a cauldron come to light
      all unwritten does not

      How can shapes and blots
      of lives steaming with pain
      and so much love be forgot

My camera trembles not
from chill of gray
first light

Confronting the Mountain

Tbilisi, 1986

Can't ride the funicular
to the mountaintop,
a poem coming on
like a cold.

Incline too steep,
cable car creaks,
lines fray. If I sneezed
they'd split.

If the lead car
slipped from its tracks,
soared on its own
across those snowed peaks

would the rest follow?
This crowd at the base
is rooted on solid ground.
Safer to stay with them.

Safer to write the poem.
If my head starts to twirl,
my stomach to clench,
I can jump out.

Yet in this land
a poem can be
more dangerous,
land you in jail—

Certain Archetypal Encounters

The basso was Hungarian, the tenor, Greek,
the pianist was Roma, a Rumanian or Turk.

While the basso bowed, passed his beret around,
horn and piano played *Romance*, Adolphe Blanc.

Grog the drink, low the lights, the evening was enhanced
by mystery and music to intensify a dangerous romance:

who might wait behind the drapes, maroon velour,
what listening devices hide among the *petit-fours*?

Mornings downstairs while the café still was shut, I've spied
the concierge untangling lines, sprinkling pots, hiding wires.

Tonight we pour our dregs of grog into the pot. Might
any bugs short-circuit? But no sizzle, no flash of light.

Next table over, two men in dark hats, dark overcoats,
check their watches, sip their *grog*, and scribble notes.

Thus my guest discusses weather and an antique balladeer
centuries ago who seldom dared to sing his own songs here.

My guest stands, gives me a mournful kiss. The men
at the next table stand, herd him out the door. Then

the basso bows, thrusts forth his beret and steps up his rounds.
To mask sounds, musicians bang out waltzes, Strauss, Johann.

Sisterhood: Mothers of Prisoners

For K & D & X

In another century and land
Akhmatova queued up beyond
the Kresty jail in Leningrad
to pass through that grilled hatch
with essential bribes for guards
parcels for her son, dissident, detained.

A wrinkled woman recognized
the poet, in a whisper asked,
"And this, can you put into words?"
"I can," Akhmatova replied.
She went home to her meager flat
and wrote her epic *Requiem*.

You and I line up outside *these* walls,
first must be approved, tip the guards,
to send our parcels through the iron grill
to a wayward child, now locked inside.
Could we have rescued…?

May we at least find
uncertain solace in our sisterhood.

With Mandelstam

*Osip Mandelstam's "...moral and spiritual courage
during years of poverty, censorship, internal exile,
and ultimately illness ending in a lonely death..."*

Reginald Gibbons

Though poets are better off dying *here*
in this land, we are familiar with internal exile
and frantic searches for solitude

and all of us everywhere
alone or surrounded
by weeping family

or chortling prison guards
know we will die alone
and even if thrown in mass graves

like clichés to be exorcized
will remain alone when dead
no more need be said

In Seeming Solitude

Time alone! But no paper or pen.
Only my trickster mind, again…

    Yet Indonesia's rebel poets, exiled
    without paper or pen to desert isles,

    did they write with twigs at low tides
    on sand till surf censored their lines?

    In jungles, might captives slip off to write
    on mud in monsoons on a moonless night?

    In Siberian jails, to write on snow and ice?
    Solzhenitsyn said: "Toilet paper sufficed."

    Mandelstam's jail mates learned his lines
    and men who survived their confinement

    smuggled out his poems in their heads,
    kept his work live after he was dead…

Are my lazy mind, seeming liberty,
pencils, laptops, forms of captivity?

I have told others "write with your blood…"
On a stone? I prick a finger, and a flood—

Elisavietta Ritchie

The Traveler Stops in a Hamlet at Dusk
And the Headman Answers his Questions

No, the mountains between our clans
are not tall or rugged or sharp
as mountains are meant to be.

Their language rougher than ours,
they mispronounce our words,
malign our gods. Like their dogs,

they slink around, sully our land,
steal our fowl, our sheep, our goats,
and worst of all, our girls—

Mothers don't know from which clan
is their baby: sired by one of us or of *them*?
The children unsure of their provenance,

our village elders grandparent all.
Each house has an extra cot,
every table holds extra bowls.

So it has always been, my friend, so it may
always be. You will find the hay in *our*
stable dry, a soft enough place to sleep.

On the Cusp of a War

Cyprus, December 1963

Carob leaves aligned on twigs,
feathers on horny quills,
pattern half-buried columns
leftover from ancient wars.

Like leathery daggers, curved pods
long and flat and tough,
hold beans like mahogany limas
and shed an odd chocolate scent.

The baby inside me kicks
as if to escape from his own
elliptical pod and emerge
with a Grecian greeting, *Elah!*

Gunfire from the far side
of this pastured hill
shatters the carob tree,
scatters pods on the dirt.

You Invite Me to Visit Your Coliseum But—

Lions lurk in the wings, spring on unwilling contestants—

In Fifth Grade History, a safe distance in time
and geography, we bemoaned the cruelty
of ancient Romans who cheered from high tiers,

and we mourned the misused lion.
We grew up, learned: men always train
to slaughter whatever Foe of the Month.

George Bellows' *Boxers* showed the zeal
of men taking it out on each other,
the spectators' hunger for knockouts, blood.

Men herd themselves into stadiums to watch
live amputations and stonings. Or on the piazza
bonfires and hangings are their entertainment.

The same throughout the Bible for millennia:
young David dispatched Goliath with a pebble,
King Saul ordered the foreskins of 20,000 Philistines.

What do you do with 20,000? Butcher shop? Lions?
Any lion would be a benevolent bystander
among Rome's pussycats in the rubble.

Meanwhile, women wrap bandages, wind shrouds,
readjust veils, raise our babies. All together
in the arena, we cheer ourselves on.

Wet red sand clogs our throats, lions clear their own.

"I Wish I Could Pray," Says Tatyana

Pray to God to resolve
one more war on His watch?

Which side of which battlefield?
Which war? A selection out there.

We can only cheer on
each our own armies,

somehow try to pray.

II WEAVERS

Spiders
>> *filter in, lace up*
>>>> *my windows and eaves,*
>>>>> *would keep winter out*
>>>>>> *with fragile shadows,*
>>>>>>> *dusty thread,*

needle

Old Masters, We Love Skulls

We perch skulls
on linen cloths,
folds tinged indigo,

set skulls on stones
outside a hermit's cave

or stack skulls
in pyramids like friends
bent close to decipher
archaic or forbidden texts
by candlelight.

The cranium bare,
no artifice, illusion,
we can reinvent
the hapless bloke's
character and life.

The eyes we paint
haunt galleries but
empty sockets, infinite
dark wells, also stare.

Sinners, paupers, monks,
provide skulls cheap,
need no model's fee.

Skulls don't chatter,
criticize, seduce,
break pose or sneeze,
don't seem to need
to eat or pee.

As models,
skulls ideal.

Elisavietta Ritchie

Long Yellow-Brown Field, Dark Red Barn

For Suzanne

Your painting is not the field
or the barn. Only an image.

My poem is not field
or barn or canvas.

Thinkers forever mull
over The Thing Itself,

Thing's shadow, copy, painting,
photograph once these invented.

Dark will swallow
the picture on the wall

but neither the field itself
nor barn vanish.

Paintings should last
for millennia unless

the gallery catch fire,
floods rise too high,

or missiles from inevitable
wars destroy everything:

gallery, field and barn,
artist, poet and town.

Then only viewers'
untrustworthy minds,

unreliable poets' lines,
might preserve

canvas or field and barn
for a time.

The Potentially Unfulfilled Crimson Hen

For Megan

The crimson hen sits on a nest
of brown leaves, or is that straw?
We don't know if she sits on
an egg, as logical for a hen.

The artist who with swift brush strokes
created her while I watched, may not
have thought to paint an egg before
she painted the hen to sit on the nest.

Yet was this hen programmed to incubate
an egg, even a painted one? We don't know.
The artist completed her sketch of the hen,
moved on to paint two hummingbirds in flight.

Girl with Grapes, **Artist Anonymous**

The model speaks

I was washing the grapes
by hand in a wooden tub
when a young man whose name
I cannot recall directed a green
garden hose at the fruit and at me.

Summer days hot when Monsieur X
painted my portrait, did the young man
aim the water to cool me
and so I'd have to take off
and wring out my dress?

Something sexual there?
Was this the case then?
I was 16, I think.

I study the painting now,
inhale the fragrance of grapes,
taste wine from a previous vintage,
recall my curls slipped from my crimson scarf
as the young man with curls damp as mine—

I recall the delights of stripping grapes
into the vat while he sluiced them,

but also the dangers
as gold-and-black hornets swarmed
and oh! how those hornets stung—

And oh, how he soothed my skin
with kisses of newly-pressed wine…

Adolphe Blondheim: *The Decoration*

The widow speaks:

Now I am widow who never was wife.
They present me a medal destined for him—
What use is beribboned silver in graves?

My fleeting lover must have told
his captain my girlhood name,
where to find me. Here, after years…

Our dark-eyed boy will inherit this
souvenir from a father he never knew,
who never acknowledged him…

He holds an enormous glass jug
floated ashore from the ship
that bore his father away

to fight in some stranger's war
for a stranger's cause, for adventure
or to escape his debts. But I have mine.

Our daughter picked oranges to fill a bowl
for we are hungry, but the artist wants
oranges for color, our faces so pale.

Maroon, my dress, yet looks black
as my hair, as my life. What *lady* works
as a model? I've kept on my clothes.

Did my darling abandon others in other lands?
But he has acknowledged *us*.
It is *we* who continue to grieve.

Quick-Change Artists

The caterpillar
on my doorstep
may have aspired

to my hospitality
and will soon show off
magnificent wings—

I'm not fooled by the curves
and curls; know, despite
the vaunted social behavior,

only a Tent Caterpillar*
whose future a dusty and dull
Gray-Brown Snout Moth.

The fiercer fat green red-horned
Tomato Caterpillar becomes
an elegant Five-Spotted Hawkmoth.**

Malacosoma americanum
***Manduca quinquemaculata*

Lunatic Moons

I extol full moon nights
how even if storms
bandage the sky
my energy roars,
new work billows forth—

"*We* dread full moons,"
says the RN over our tea.
"That's when the loonies
tend to hit the ER."
She studies me sideways.

I slap down a ten
for unfinished pastries,
wish her good night shifts,
run home through twilight
crazed with flames.

In time I'll go blind
so while the lunatic moon
crowns from the sea
must write fast
snatch at stars—

The Famous Poet Limps to the Stage with Her Cane

For Maxine

each step each breath
another slash of pain

the numbing pills that bring
kind thunderclouds into her brain
must be eschewed this night

her night of glory and of pain
of need to bow and smile
in gratitude for celebration of her life
her love for critters, forests, lovers
and books by many a sage

her gratitude for any crumpled page
she wrote while in that torture cage
that held her bones together for a while

so this night of need to bow and smile
give thanks for seldom tardy admiration
she hides her thoughts of ending pain
with blessed death

to bless the rest of us below the stage
who laud her fame

try not to see her pain

No Similes, No Metaphors

For G

Ignore well-meaning friends who say,
"Your grief will pass. Move on, away."

They don't move on, our beloved dead.
They move *with* us, and hang around,

keep watch despite seeming absence,
they console us, counsel, reminisce.

Not fickle, we are staying, hence
bless our loyalty, our persistence.

Our memories can no longer fade.
We still love you. Don't be afraid.

Drifters to Oceans

Why do most personae
in my short stories
want to end up in an ocean?

Concern to enrich
the diets of fish?
Raise the sea level?

Or solve the dilemma
for others of whether
to dig or to burn?

Both labor intensive,
take time and space,
leave a mess on land.

Bones at sea also take
time to dissolve:
question of temperature.

Whatever the reason,
my characters tend
to steer for the water's edge.

So let them head for the beach,
dive, ride the high rollers,
dance on the surf—

The Publisher of My First Book Notes: "Such Sense of Death!"

Of course. Age eight we learned to sail:
from the dock leap aboard, scrub guano off decks,
slide mainsail out boom, inch top up the mast,
hoist mainsail and jib, cleat them fast,
uncleat hawser, tighten but don't cleat sheets,
cast off, slalom around boats in the harbor.

When out far enough from the marina,
if following winds auspicious, raise spinnaker
but hang onto gunwale and sheets.
Skate over the waves
like that famed bat-from-hell
grown-ups must not hear us cite.

Of course we intend to return to home port.
Near the dock we'll head into the wind,
sidle up without crashing, grab pilings, cleat
hawser/uncleat lines/lower sails/shake/dry/furl
all at the same time. We will dry and bag sails,
put the boat to bed, then ourselves safely at home.

Yet a squall could engulf our fragile craft—
Jonah's whale could gulp us—
And as with generations of our forbearers
the hurricane bound to drown us all
could finish us off before our time
or long after…

So I Wear the Shoes of the Dead

Bought at Thrifts, cheapies
But they're broken in, not as stiff
As their previous owners now
Soles and souls well-worn if
To some of you, creepy.

Their stories people my head
Secrets they did not allow
Their families to know
I will rewrite anyhow
Anyhow, they are dead.

III EXPLORERS

One huge gray spider
spins a new web every day
between the same boulders

On Googling the Word
Nu·mi·nous *(adj \ ˈnü-mə-nəs, ˈnyü-\)*
While Finishing Last Night's
Leftover *Choucroute Garnie*

Humble sauerkraut with low-fat turkey kielbasa plus onion and
      parsnips yet after searching for the precise definition of
      that word "numinous" ignored since Lit 101 and now
      re-encountered

now I understand how my scatter of
      caraway fruits (erroneously called <u>seeds</u>, says Wikipedia)
      juniper berries (female <u>seed cones</u>, not true berries but cones
         though found in Egyptian tombs, most likely came
         from Greece, also says Wikipedia)
      peppercorns (seeds of berries from the Malabar coast of
         India; I needed no Wiki to teach me
         about peppercorns)

Nor does it take academia to explain how my sprinkling exotic
      berries/seeds over what in childhood I called spoiled
      cabbage with anemic carrots translucent onions and garlic
      that made me cry

Elevated the casserole to a mystical dish and spiritual experience
      categorized as *numinous* though one should not question
      what stuffs sausage or which divine spirit mystified us

To find definitions Online I bushwhacked through thickets
of pop-up advertisements
      for flat or fat bellies and sapphire rings
      granted little numinous about most bellies
      though fasting brings visions

Guy Wires

Sapphires have a luminous/numinous quality
  are full of mental and physical healing capacities
  upholding of chastity and protective against sorcery
  so says Online and more

Sapphires kill snakes on impact
  help one connect to the universe
  open one's internal and spiritual self
    to the powers of the universe
  increase communication with
  spirit guides sometimes known as angels

Sapphires also cure ulcers
  so says it Online

Now I've plumbed numinous and luminous I may be able to
  appraise in a proper academic or pedagogical manner those
  instants of both or either long accepted as ephemeral gifts
  from whatever Divinity

Such as
  platinum sheen on waves before a squall
  startling song of migratory wrens
  love-call of Australian mourning doves more mellifluous
    than American white moths over cabbage plants
    although it should not land tree-of-life pattern in
    bisected red cabbage
  onyx gleam on cormorants
  dragonfly perched on a crab trap at ebb tide and the
    consequent haiku
  Concord grape in the fingers of a
    would-be-if-things-were-different lover
  Concord grape in the fingers of a really-true lover

Even leftover feathers from the hapless turkey
  ground into that sausage

Given the serendipity that the slaughter process and processing
occurred far away
      so I don't feel responsible for turkey-murder
      as for three long-ago chickens age twelve I personally had
         to murder pluck eviscerate but did not eat
      the numinous result being decades of vegetarianism

I can step with more confidence into the jungles of scholarly
      dissection of words and of poultry.

Heidegger at the Breakfast Table

You won't descend to our green plain,
insist we hike up rocky trails
at dawn to reach your mountain.

You question our existence—never mind.
Our guts growl, so we know we are alive,
scratched bloody after our rough climb.

You turn us off with dumb conundrums.
We're well aware of limits to our lives,
why waste our time with *insoluble* problems?

You wear a peasant shirt to prove your roots,
thick boots which tracked in leaves—
you should have left them on the stoop.

We heard wolves as we came—we hope
once breakfast done, you'll lead us through your grove
to well-marked trails and safer slopes.

But you won't let us eat in peace,
demand we think on *thinking* though we starve—
We think about your promised feast.

Your "feast" is blue-green bread!
Your knife first slaughtered boar,
hacks hunks of cheese like heads.

No thanks! But lest we faint and fall
we'll snitch those berries from your thorns…
Tart pebbles…*Something* beats *nothing at all*.

Preliminary Experiments

1.
All these men who describe their first
filched drinks or binges with booze,
what happened or did not, age 17,

certain experiments deliberate,
or liquor suddenly caught up with them—
Big mistake, Mama, I swear!

Age six I swiped my mother's Lucky Strikes,
but coughed and choked on smoke,
gave up butts that Lent and ever.

My mother alcoholic, I realized:
liquor in the genes,
booze in the blood, best abstain.

2.
Sailing all day in an open boat
leaves a sailor dry. Men's
confessions emphasize the *I*:

thus *I* returned from port
to find in fullest swing
the neighbors' shindig.

The usual smelly bottles but
also a big bowl brimming
with fruity fizzy punch.

Five cups quenched my thirst
much better than what
school served from a can.

Walking home through cedars,
across adjoining lawns,
the green beneath my feet

sped past amazingly fast.
I realized: *my first drunk...*
Quick quick, write, describe—

I scribbled through one
whole yellow pad all night,
white heat and all that.
Isn't this what writers do?
Who cares about penmanship
or writing all over the page?

Morning. How to decipher
my earth-shaking manuscript?
Cannot untangle a line.

The Thing about Drinking

to get to sleep, or whatever excuse: you
are two, aware you're aware of the split.

As Watcher this freezing night
you observe yourself dash rum
in milk, warm till almost too hot,
describe how Drinker savors
every risky drop…

Under full moons we write best.
Tonight just a slice to inspire.

Look! You're scribbling between
someone else's lines!

This was all the paper on hand,
typed both sides, not one blank page.
What was written before,
we cannot efface.
We've not even birthed
a bona fide palimpsest.

Theories of dual-selves hardly new,
de Maupassant springs to mind:
his *artiste* in the circle's center while
at the edge to spy on himself,
and beyond the circumference
to watch himself spy on himself.

So Drinker and Watcher spin off a Third.
Disparate dissolute Selves in a literate mob,
we live a tri-partite existence.

If not unique, the process remains of interest.
Let's plunge on…Another nip
in the interest of science.

That author whose opus we swiped
demands center stage:
words seep through paper and pores
to influence what we think we observe.

Turns out: an Old Self thought discarded.
"Rank duplicity!" chorus all Four.
Despite sludge in our heads,
we write till the sun melts leftover
slivers of moon and of ice.

Self One now spoons honey into a cup
for coffee Self Two tries to brew…

From outside, Self Three peers
through the window. *You've overcooked
the oatmeal, burned all the bread!
And it's too cold out here!*

And with *Four* Selves to feed,
charred crumbs won't suffice.

Self Four wants aspirin for headache,
wants to forget last night.

But all four Selves recall every sip,
decipher each splash on the page,
scatter crumbs for the birds,
pour rum over chocolate babka cake.

Emergency Alert Systems

Cramps twist my legs in screaming knots. Mushrooms! Hidden in
tonight's soup at Mama Lucia's! Mushrooms poison me. Must drive
miles to the Emergency Room

This is a restricted area Police have been called Leave An unknown
microphone beyond our woods repeats *Leave the area immediately
This is a restricted area Police have been called*

Alone in the house by the cove but for one half-tabby stray
who, while loving (when hungry), can neither share my sense of
responsibility nor dial 911. Go! She won't let

Did intruders slip through our woods, hide in the marsh beyond
the span of our security light? Must put on shoes, check the
neighborhood, leave! 3:15 a.m.? It's raining torrents

This is a restricted area The cat won't go out, or let me by to open
the door. Does she sense an intruder? Intruders? Animals intuit…
Police have been called Leave the area immediately This

What set off alarms up the hill? Raccoons with their tiny black
hands? Which windows latch properly? Side door stays unlocked,
key long lost. Raccoons could pick these locks

Four small lights from trailers across the cove reassure: if I
scream, someone will launch a boat, zoom over. *Leave the area
immediately…*Or is it, *"Do not leave?"* Hard to decipher

Or are trailer folks focused on poker, TV, love by the water, absent,
or drunk? Would cops find our dirt road through the woods? Would
intruders?*…restricted area, Leave immed*

The moon, two-thirds of itself, reflects on the cove. Night is
cold. No boats in the cove *Leave the area immediately…This is a
restricted area Police have been called Leave the area immedia*

What if someone up there is hurt? Needs my help? Rain lighter,
cramps subsiding, I should go up the hill and find out—*This is a
restricted area, police have been called. Leave*

Some individuals are put on earth not to act, but to bear witness…
Truisms pundits and poets reiterate to avoid active roles of trying
to rescue the earth, avoid danger…*Lea*

*Leave the area immediately Police have been called This is a
restricted area…Leave Leave Leave*   Toadstools, scarlet, gold,
death-white, push through wet soil, surround, block my path

Notes for a Poem on Exploring Myself

Time to go inside
I've hid outside too long

Must risk discovering
still inside my womb
a six-toed Tatar child
curled beside a blonder embryo
ready if
his number should come up instead

Risk surprising in the antechamber
as in Penelope's hall
assemblies of alien sperm
of infinite variety

Or inside ribs
a dozen hearts like suckling pigs
each with a different beat
pigs nuzzling different veins

Or inside breasts
orgiastic cells
multiplying exponentially

Or finding in my skull
marshmallow whip
with cyclamates

And tapeworms everywhere
measuring shrouds

Time to surface

But Ariadne's thread
writhes in hopeless knots

Crossing the Dunes

1.
I leave the so-called Waterfront Hotel
with its pleasant confusions
of people known for the moment the way
they are encountered in dreams.

The Southern Ocean gleams just beyond
the expanse of orange-beige dunes.
"Nice beach," people say, "over there."

Desperate to swim in this heat,
I clamber up berms of pebbly sand,
slide down trails, climb more dunes.

Illusion of proximity…

How many canyons cut
between the road and sea!
Each step an avalanche of sand.

A man drenched with dust and sand,
he resembles my old geology prof,
emerges from the next dune, blocks my path.

"Far hike out there," he warns,
then lies down on the sand, closes his eyes.
I stretch out at his feet, only awake
at the meow of my anxious white cat.

That *was* a dream after all.
What message might it convey?

2.
Alone I crossed *genuine* dunes of white sand
in South Australia: the Southern Ocean
lapped the edge of Nullarbor Desert,
This bona fide beach would be near.

An hour later, dune after slippery dune,
I stared at tumults of undertow.
Surf, rolling north from Antarctica's cliffs,
banged icebergs against my blistered toes.
Fatigue, cold, thirst for lost water bottles....

3.
Up Northwest Australia's warmer coast
another *real* afternoon, again alone,
I set off for the Indian Ocean, glimpsed
beyond herds of bony long-horns
grazing on saw grass, prickly brush.

Miles of pastureland, seared, maroon...
A disconsolate river cut me off...
I veered onto tidal flats: slimy clay, sinkholes for miles...

At last! The sea! At last! To swim at last...

Big signboards warned:
BEWARE! RIPTIDES RISKY!
BOX JELLYFISH LETHAL! SHARKS! CROCODILES!

I limped back inland, took shortcuts, lost my way...
somehow at last found a road,
got home, I guess...

Searching Hong Kong for Chocolate

July 1977

The Chinese word for chocolate
is indecipherable.

I hunt through pungent streets
molasses-thick…
Any chocolate imported must
have melted away in the heat.

In a tall hotel, booked alone,
caught in the interim between
two husbands, two lands,
two lovers distant and dying,
I must find chocolate—

Or else a doppelganger,
to find poets my business here.

Everyone here in shipping and trade.
Few speak my language or know my name,
though I am here trying to make one,
poem by poem, but at the moment out
to discover chocolate.

To find chocolate, or a poet,
would be like sighting—while lost
in Mongolian desert wastes—
a chocolate-pistachio sundae made
with milk of a yak, the whole mound
drenched with dark chocolate sauce.

My tongue is bound in splints and rags.
Loneliness wraps me in my blue sarong.

On My Own

1
Water in the Coffeemaker Frozen

Park ranger leaves, Maintenance cleans, cop checks locks and security light, drives off. I twist my happenstance key to the MENS. In the dimness inside, I insert coffeemaker plug in the socket, press a button, and return to my tent.

Six a.m. every day before Maintenance comes, machine turns itself on. I enter, squirt soap, scrub head to toe, shower, dry off, dress, coffee's perked. Nothing works today! Can't drink coffee till showered, then eat what breakfast I find.

Toilets won't flush, faucets won't spurt and splatter, lights won't light. Security bulb gray. This morning, all frozen? Electricity fail last night? Not even a dab-bath. My towel is my extra blanket, at least this stays dry.

My talkative tabbies, like the park's foxes and deer, grew winter coats. Mine thin. We all huddle close to the scruffy ground, wind can't whip our undersides. I crawl home to my tent with this precious, useless, coffeemaker someone left

in that dirty red pickup parked in the lot. Truck hasn't budged in a fortnight. Must be abandoned, but minus keys. Can't hot wire, damn it…No way to drive, sample packets of Instant at Wendy's, Super6, McDs. Cannot even hitch a ride.

Are all morning's chirpers, honkers and peepers too cold to twitter? Winter nights tundra swans whistle but must have flown to another cove. No herons overfly with a croak, geese still asleep on their fields. As if after a blizzard, odd quiet.

I peer out the flap. Nothing moves outside the tent, or inside. Even the mouse who teases the cats won't creep from her Spam-can nest wedged between tent pole and spoke. Too cold today to hike

to the library where I check Internet, find leftover snacks,
sometimes half-eaten oranges, crackers in baggies, jerky to share
with the cats. Library supposed to exist for the public—Won't open
without heat or light.

But Monday a kindly old-timer forgot a crushed box of doughnuts
with icing! In my sleeping bag, warm with both cats, I'll eat my
fortuitous bounty, read my overdue books, if ink and my fingers
thaw, write my own…So I am, I exist, alive.

2
On the Beach

I don't desecrate any Stars and Stripes! Hell, no! I don't let it touch
the ground.

Yet nights by the ocean turn chilly. Homeless, penniless, wardrobe-
less since my wife called me "Nutty since Nam, Irrational since
Iraq, Abnormal after Afghanistan," and threw me out with a
sandwich. Still conscientious, I left her whatever money.

So a Wounded Warrior I, Wandering minstrel with my lute, but I
don't often starve.

Wasteful good citizens leave unfinished picnics by the Boardwalk,
beers only half-drunk if flat. A gull, dusty angel, swipes a hot dog
from a child, drops it in my lap. One frequent surf-caster shares
surplus flounder or striper we cook over his Sterno.

And I have discovered dumpsters.

At times I sing for my supper. A lute's won a lady for centuries,
they linger late, curl up—All I need say is *Guide me, please,*
through dark labyrinths of dunes—Today's gals prefer Pop and
Rock to Old French., but claim to love my baby face.

A comb from the LADIES slicks my hair like Elvis Presley.

They'll open more than their picnic baskets. But don't worry, I
stay clean: I swim. Jellyfish sting but stings dissipate. One outdoor
shower by the MEN's works, at least in summer. Razors left in the
MEN'S are sharp enough.

Sunset, beach cops lower our flag, stash in a cupboard behind
changing rooms.

Picnickers and patrollers departed, I jimmy the lock (a useful talent
learned Stateside). Our flag covers me, or us, all night, keeps out

sand fleas. First light, before sunrise silvers the ocean, the flag is back in the cupboard, not a wrinkle.

Yours and mine, that good old Made-in-China American flag.

I deserve it. Fought under it, almost died under it, kept at bay our nation's foes. I miss Asian cuisine, but learned to survive on little food, lotta brains. So yes, I am surviving, thank you, at least till December.

3
That Little Pink Rubber Piglet

Tossed onto the scruffy lawn. Extra-high tide? Hurricane surf?
Floods bring planks, antique flasks, Styrofoam, unmentionables,
from upriver in return for stuff floods swipe from shore.

No serious weather in recent news. Storms ago, this kid's toy
must have got stuck in a swamp, river muck, or in a far sand
castle-with-barnyard built on a summertime beach.

Hard rubber, two inches snout to tail, inch-and-a-quarter high,
Lips leer, smirk or grin as if oinking for food, puddles, rescue from
butchers, or as rare piglets get raised as spic-and-span pets, petting.

Dirty, this piglet. Swipes with a soapy rag no improvement.
One whole week soak in a bowl with detergent, then a scrubber,
clean only a bit. So be it: piglet remains a gray-dappled pink.

The banality of him grabs me in the gut—or *her?* Can't guess
gender: this critter has neither nipples of budding sows nor
nascent equipment of boar/barrow/stag to shock.

Were it a miniature horse, cow or goat from an Old Macdonald
Farm Set, child's items dropped in the bilge or washed overboard
or in, I'd merely pass it on to Goodwill. This *thing* is all piglet.
Solid.

What child young enough to bring toys aboard would be allowed
on a boat while Daddy is busy fishing? No season for crabbers,
just hunters where toddlers banned from the scene, or should be.

Was a waterside garden littered with toys gulped by the sea?
House and child too? Programmed to wash up on *this* shore?
Nothing, surely, so ominous…Mythical fish may barter for freedom.

Trained birds—carrier pigeons, falcons who nab sparrows en route,
Noah's propitious Dove—can fly in with a message. But a fake
piglet?

What omen inherent in this mysterious river gift? And why to *me…*

4
Mid-October, Water Cold

Dolphins, seals, sea lions, those distant heads?
Walruses strayed?

Most mammals have headed south
or never came this far north.

Walls of waves engulf them again
and again,
more waves blanket the jetty, would fracture the blocks
of slippery boulders heaped here to stop
sea from gulping beach—

High rollers out there.

Three men emerge from exploding foam—

They attach feet to boards, slip, reattach,
skim the swells, pirouette,
somersault over and over—
vanish...
Brash gamblers in surf!

Perhaps they will reappear.

I'd be elated, afraid...

This is the way to live!

This is the way to die.

I should wade out, try a board—

Sleep People

Before my finally-asleep they come, odd blobs,
odd balls who hover over my insomniac bed…

Gender? Hard to define, cannot see below
any waist to check out. Sex isn't the point.

Unfamiliar, unsubstantial, yet out to control,
they gesture, converse—God, how they talk!

Can't hear a word. Mimes of a sort?
Must confront shapes for details…

How to survive any sleep they might yield…
They admonish: *Do something other than sleep!*

I embark on writing a pivotal book—
Before I resolve any plot, they fade…

Cecelia, Dancer, Retired

from Torn Pages Discovered
in an Abandoned Shopping Bag,
Subtitles Apparently Added

Cecelia Was Born in Chicago And This Imprinted on Her Life

They say I was conceived in a snow storm by a sailor stuck in the
ice. He walked
off over the lake like Jesus on frozen seas. My mother never gave
her right name.

Age six, trying to find my father, I tunneled through snow drifts
and created snow
angels on Lake Shore Drive, traffic mired in snow, and so was I.

Sent to school, I exploded the Chemistry Lab. The teacher, a
scientist fled from Berlin,
forgave me, kindled my love for science, and for men with accents
and stories to tell....

Invited to sing before the whole school, I sang. Everyone laughed.
Never sang again.
But I learned to write, experiment, dance on the stage, think on my
feet, and discover

logical solutions: When the last bridge toll costs two bucks and you
must nickel-and-
dime it but you're a dime short, you dive in.

Cecelia Experiences Many Reversals of Fortune

If you are beautiful and love dance, you dance even when no
longer beautiful and your
fortunes disappear in the breeze, like tiny slips of fortunes Chinese
cookies envelop...

Like old lovers. But one still sends me
scarlet roses for Valentine's Day.

Cecelia's New Life Rag

A stranger's kitchen cutlery,
a rollaway with broken springs,
locked cupboards with another's things.

Each night I wake (nights when I sleep)
dry-mouthed yet find upon my tongue
like dust the taste of borrowed rum...

Only my white angora cat...

A New Lover Throws Cecelia a Birthday Party, with Measurable Gifts

They gave me sets of aluminum cups...
 But I measure everything in my palm.

Then, locked in plastic caskets too tough
to cut, serrated knives, ill-tempered steel.
Could they know I'm known for flipping blades?
Next party I'll pass a knife to every guest,
test who flips best, drips the most.

At last the perfect gift— a tin of unbagged tea!
They must have known I like it loose and hot...

Cecelia, Dancer, Suffers Drawbacks But Makes Lemonade

Eye swollen shut, no scarves will veil.
Can't be seen today or go to work.
They'll ask, "He at it again?"

If I stay home, only dumb TV—
sitcoms, detective, boxing – all
where guys with black eyes
end up on their duffs.

Or I'd have to clean closets: clear
gowns tattered from years
in the spotlights of hell…

Ah! My coverall crème, lipstick,
powder, mascara, rouge,
eye shadow so the both eyes match.

I'll make up, doll up, return to the streets,
to my subterranean lives, celebrate
my dark mysterious eyes…

But beware! One-eyed, my mother-of-pearl
custom-made Ladysmith can still shoot
and shoot straight, and I get what I want.

Cecilia, Dancer, Maintains
Communications on the Job

Too hot for my ermine muff. I used to hide
my cell phone inside the satin lining, ripped.
No pockets in my veils, I slip it in my bra…
Always on in case my agent calls, or you.

I hurry to the tavern where they asked for me
to wiggle my notorious hips again on stage.
I do forget who called me when—

Before my gigs, you'd fill my glass with gin,
afterwards my bra with chocolate cake to take home…

You always liked my breasts.
These breasts which nursed six babies, triplets twice:
I littered like a sow. But growing, scattered, kids
forget to phone. Sundays now I mostly spend alone.

My breasts warm up the cell phone.
When the Vibrato's on, watch out—

Come out, Honey, watch! I still swirl my bum!
My magenta tassels twirl in all directions while
tarnished sequins catch rainbows in the lights—

When lights are low, smoke dims people's sight,
my wrinkles, damn them, do not show.

Rain falls thick! I need a shower anyway.
So, your same old dancing girl away I go—

Cecelia Attempts to Provide An Unexpected Visitor with Hospitality

Sleepless night. Rosy-fingered clammy-palmed dawn:
Strange man in my hall! Skinny. Wool cap half over face.
I should be terrified—

First must feed my angora cat, claws bloody my shins.

You insomniac like me? I ask. Blue pills? I'm a druggie too.
Wine, aspirin & heart beats of a warm man
cold nights don't cure insomnia.

What you in for? Break out? Or snatch a pass?
I won belts in karate, could inflict pain on your privates.

Care for coffee? Cinnamon buns? Fridge.
Sugar in jar, we have ants. You want half-&-half?
Out of half-&-half.

Sorry, you say, I gotta rob another house,
Who do you know who might have half-&-half?

Cecelia Writes A Letter To Her Heart

Old Pump, you haven't skipped a beat of late,
all those years of dancing weren't enough.
Snowmelt from climbed Himalayas trickled till it filled
the River Styx but not yet drains my arteries.

So I will dance till sunrise, jog up Everest—
keep up with me if you can. Please try.

Cecelia Tackles the Avenue Again

Must extricate this coat, fragrant with camphor,
forty years old, bought at a thrift: gray herringbone,
finest wool, same button gone, same pocket holes.

Falls to my heels! *I've...shrunk.* No matter. It and I
worked then, will still...A bright orange scarf a flame...

Nobody else wearing coats in this wind. Pneumonia weather!

How noisy now these crowded streets where I'd meet
my lovers at street corners, corner cafes—those days, they paid.

These men today might have been my lovers then...
Now scruffy as curs...they shuffle and limp...Hair
grayed or gone, they've changed shades, or vanished...

Then one man holds the door of a new café
where I remember a tavern. So I smile, enter...

And he disappears...

Cecelia Faces Realities in the Mini-Mall Parking Lot, 6 a.m.

Yeah, that's me, (or I?) you see
dragging bags, one black, four white,
heavy, all my lives inside.

Past week was cold and wet and so was I.
Now sun and warmth. Up the street magnolias
bloom pink and white as my babies' cheeks—
Leather leaves and soggy petals make me slip.

No cars yet, there's space in the lot, weather's fair.
Gym jocks begin aerobics, handstands—long legs
bicycle the air as if to travel through the stratosphere.
I barely walk, though someone's radio makes me want
to leap onstage again. I must be careful not to trip.

No dumbells for me. My bags are weights enough—

Balls? I'd pitch them to the kids—None here yet,
Mean kids call me a *hag*...

I circumvent the puddles where spilled gasoline
swirls rainbows and reflects a hungry sky.

The market's setting bargains out... No
bargains these pineapples and mangoes
from tropic climes where fruit grows cheap.

I wear my blanket, guard my bags...forget
what's packed in each. Clothes? Few'd fit.
Food? Gone or stale. If paper, pencils, pens—
My pens leaked, blackened everything, then dried.

My magpie eyes no longer pick up words
but spot half a hotdog in a bin—

Best park my bags beside the café chairs—

I don't need *things*, dumbbells or shiny spheres.
Need—anyone—if anyone now needed me.

Those worn-out tires might pillow me tonight.
I'm glad for sunshine, and an empty bench.

Dance Steps

We are waltzing into a future
of glass, expertly ground,
beneath our bared feet.

Machines grind glass
on every corner. Glass
sparkles rainbows,
colors forever mutating.

Shoes no help. Shards
penetrate leather and lead,
slip into the bloodstream.

At least only fatal when,
after coursing throughout
arteries, veins, even the gullet,
they finally reach the heart.

Les Bonnes Intentions à la J-P Sartre

The Dutchman, 27, after trekking Brazil
with backpack and a bunch
of addresses of friends-of-friends,
after five nights in our spare room,
discussed his thesis on Nazi doctors,
then packed for his first trip to New York.

The dark wool topcoat I'd promised because
of impending Manhattan blizzards was no
more in our attic among ball gowns, outgrown shoes,
a long-gone spouse's abandoned tuxedo.

Then I spotted two thick wool sweaters, blue,
in perfect shape, left by a tenant or ex.

"Layer these beneath your rain jacket:
when it warms up, topcoats a burden.
Extra sweaters are simpler to stuff in a pack.
You've good boots. Here's an apple—Good trip."

He kissed me three times on both cheeks, left
for the metro, cheapo bus to New York,
JFK in a week, the plane home to Holland.

Now from the seldom-breached front-hall closet
tumbles forth a silvery parka, tags attached,
an expensive gift winters ago but here spring
comes too soon for a parka so it's hung forgotten
for years and might after all never be needed.

Had it appeared yesterday, I would have mulled
whether to force this elegant garment on him,
brand new, only slightly too big for me unless
worn over two heavy sweaters....Could someday—

In New York, the blizzard closed down the city.
Here, snow falls barely an inch and soon melts.

IV FELLOWS

Admonition for a Would-Be Thought Collector

For Robert

Why try to collect them?
Do stop scrounging around.
Let thoughts take off at dusk
as cave swallows in quest
of mosquitoes, as night
herons whose beaks would pierce
full moons, drink—
with first light let them crow,
warble, whistle and chirp,
with morning fly into the sun—

Visitations: Two Vultures

I read by the cove. Large black birds overfly.
They circle back, over, lower, overshadow.
Be gone! Return for me decades hence!

They dip their wings in feathered salute,
the gray on black shoulders gleams.
They only fling shadows, for now.

They know where to return,
will tidy our world in good time.
Much business elsewhere, for now.

At First Light

six swans in the cove
trail lines in the mist
inscribe as they glide
tales of invisible rivers
beyond to discover

the swans stop
triangles of white
probe wet air
beaks plumb
unseen sand
seek bugs in the muck

I've Not Been Down That Street Before

Hardly seems a place for trysts.
Only light from stars.
Street lamps throw
jagged shadows,
then burn out.

By day, street's dim.
Bins overflow,
yet crates to hold
a boat yawn bare.

Meowls of pain—
cats, mottled fur
like dingy rags,
never purr but breed,
scrap, nab rats.

Curs fight for remains
in other alleys.
Few humans stop,
seek safer lanes.

No spy to spot exchange
of kiss or drug,
you and I could meet,
feed cats, and when
we've tamed
or drugged them
with Psilocybin,

ourselves drugged
with love,

feast upon each other
unobserved—

Two-Headed Calf in a Jar of Formaldehyde

Or was it a two-headed…*baby*…?
I was fifteen, the museum on the Mall.

Years later I check: the pickled—
whatever—and museum have vanished.

Every day now I pass pastures of steers
destined for hamburgers, sausages, steaks.

Black except one dappled with white, one
ash gray. They chew their cud all alone.

"Steer" means "young male" but this herd
unisex: some drop an occasional calf.

No two-headed sports, genetic variants.
I keep watching, watching, and counting.

Those Old Blueberries

For Antonia

You threw the whole batch in the trash
because of a few moldy berries!
One small plastic box costs five bucks.

Most berries remain wholesome enough
to save for tomorrow's breakfast…

By sunrise the boxful is fuzzy,
unhealthy gray-white, shade
of that erroneous mushroom
which landed me in the ER….

Lined up on the balcony rail
as if with Audubon Food Stamps
and the usual hard-luck tales,

cardinals, sparrows, jays,
chickadees in ski masks for holdups,
peck the wood railing raw.

I dump the whole moldy trove
purple-gray on the rail although
the heap may further rot
untouchable and untouched.

All day they go at it.

A phalanx of starlings—
I wave them off.

Catbirds flash tails and wings,
stomp claws,
shoe the others away.

Yet in this world of everywhere
evil, hunger, scant gratitude,

at least while the blueberries last
on one narrow conjunction
of balcony rail—

Visiting Hours

Nine camels keep dancing over your bed,
cavort like kittens from pillow to post,
their tiny hooves pock the freshly-starched spread,
sequins on bridles like eyes of a ghost.

They nibble your fingers, perch in your hand,
they nestle for warmth on your burning skin,
and murmur tales of a sulfurous land,
drink up all your bitter brown medicine.

Then out your hospital window they leap,
each carves a hole through the misty gray pane.
You try to pursue—The air is too steep.
We find you crashed to earth, clutching one rein.

The floor is bright red, wherever you steered.
The camels, sated, have long disappeared.

Wolf-Huggers

Susan is nuts about wolves,
can't wait to sleep in a den,
at least feed the pups.

If cross-bred with dogs, some wolf pups,
like husbands, lovers and dingoes,
become excellent pets, for a while.

Feline

I need a cat. My
Spouse categorically
Does not. No more strays!

14 May

The black cat who stole
Into my dreams last night, wants
Feeding this morning.

6 September

Cold, rain. Soaked, cat meowls.
Spouse grabs towels, kibbles…
Cat gets the red chair.

15 October

Spideresque

She hangs from the lintel,
drops to the floor, scuttles
into the laundry hamper, wicker
no barrier, entangles herself among
silk panties, black lace, raveling socks.
She breathes Chanel, Shalimar, prefers
simpler odors of woman and barnyard.
One night she will extricate from scraps
of satin and damp handkerchiefs
one lopsided blue pearl.

V CENTRAL

Should her lover drop in
spinning his gossamer yarns
she'll eat him too

On Illustrious Ancestors

Emails pour in with attachments and charts,
communiqués on and from our elegant dead
as if e-vites to virtual weddings:

Baron von This weds Baroness von That
who, to prolong the well-titled line,
bore baronettes like juvenile penguins
with unpronounceable multiple names.

We've not been invited to christenings yet
though these happened a century or two ago.

I was unsure if this story mere gossip:

Tsar Alex the First loved a lady-in-waiting,
the Court artist's beautiful daughter, aristocrat
but not royal enough to become a tsarina.

Still, they engendered a child before
he had to marry her off to a willing noble
gentleman-in-waiting who bestowed his name
and, let us hope, his love for the lady
and the impending half-kingly baby.

Research now confirms what my father related.

And that royal engendering led in a few generations
to my own patrician cousin who confided,
"…in our line, several pairs of third cousins
fell in love…" Oceans only kept us apart.

So only *his* progeny bear and pass on
those garnet drops of royal blood
now considerably watered down.

Re my future suitors, I'll consult Peerage,
and inquire about their blood types.

Blood Lines

On Martin Luther King's birthday

I've not told you, my blue-eyed children
born with hair blond and straight,
why you tan so coffee-with-cream.

You can figure fractions, genetics:
You are one-twentieth black.

Your *father* gave you those genes.
His mother's great-great-great
fell in unadvised love or mere want
with "a stunning mulatto,"
a century back in Joplin, Missouri.

His mother in her cups when she told him,
he was his when he told me. She is long gone.
Details slipped his mind before his own demise.

On *my* side we have blue-blood in buckets
check "Caucasian" for a good reason:
my father's ancestors came from the Caucasus
and of royal lineage: two forbearers wed
genuine princesses, Tatar and Turk.
Love matches so minus the ritual kidnap.

No tawny skin came down to me.
I shield my face from the sun.

We can all re-invent our pasts.
You will manage your own and add
whatever input you choose.

If you fall for a Zambian princess/prince
with glistening obsidian skin,
I will sit back, matriarchal, hide
my amber hair with a shawl.

One pumpkin-haired grandson is proof
my aberrant genes trumped your dad's.

Our Shadow Siblings

Single children, we had to invent
our doubles, invisible playmates
to jettison soon as outgrown.

They dog us for life.

From the start they strive to rival
not *us* but some neighbors' child
with the fancier trike,
later the first two-wheeler
brand new, seven gears, red.

Teachers' pets yet adored
in our classmates' cliques,
they win all the prizes.

Picked first for First Team,
they never play Third Team goalie.

They draw all the handsome boys,
later steal husbands and lovers.

My own more exciting, exotic—

But even *they* may sneak off
to my damn wayward sibling.

Oh, for sibling-cide.

Happenstances

Had I not picked up
the cat's dish outside, I'd not
have found the wren's nest
with one warm egg unbroken.

Had I not met you
I'd not have learned loving,
patience, heaven, hell.

Unknown as the Terrain of Death

The landscape of your mind, my love:
a strange and shattered battlefield
where wrecked chariots and tanks

move through the night, *are* moved,
in untidy patterns which spell out
orders in unbroken codes.

Behind the hills, green and wooded or
sere and scarred, horses with splayed hooves
toss the inflated globe off course.

Here, cloaked as an assassin I
trace your journeys, circular,
seek in vain to reach their end.

Banana Peel Love Poem

Banana from some country fraught
with heat and revolutions: a need
to peel this label off the yellow skin
flecked black as if by Magic Markers.

United Fruit and Dole load them green
into cold storage for the voyage north.
They ignore Chiquita's admonition:
Never put bananas in refrigerators!

You dislike imperfection so I edit, delete….
Can't mulch peel with alien paper glued.
My gnawed nails scrape the label off at last,
and slip the skin into the compost bin.

Inside's unblemished, alabaster white, cold.
This knife is sharp, could cut a finger off!
I slice the red-flecked fruit into your breakfast bowl
and serve it with your coffee, hot as love.

Wind Power: Cyclonic

Thumps, thumps! Gales rips off old branches and new—Too dark to see—Too cold to go out—Snowflakes mix with hail—Hope no branches hit the new windows—Trees could fall and cave in the old roof—Already the ceiling leaks—

But you're over-spooked by the howling, my love…The big oaks still stand, limbs hold firm despite the hurricane wind. Our twelve slender Georgia pines, only sway and bend so survive as did Robert Frost's "Birches."

You move your car to the open meadow. In Hurricane Isabel, seven trees fell over our access lane, and like that flood, blocked escape. Come morning I'll walk up the hill to see, should I locate the power saw, check how much gasoline.

We may lose our power, normal in storms. I fill empty jars, bottles and jugs, find candles, matches, use up what's in the fridge, cook a stew while the stove works, find paper bowls, shower while water still flows, try again to connect on the Internet—

If in Darwin, we'd rush to a cinderblock cyclone shelter. Under this shaking house muddy crawl space, plumbing pipes, black snakes. These winter in our attic as do raccoons if their nests get tossed from the pine, we're closest safe house for critters.

Chinese also hate wind, harbinger of troubles: diseases, ill tidings, floods. Yet this is life, we live inside it, every day brings some risk, we must adapt as our ancestors did to vagaries of weather and love—

The roaring continues, more clunks and thuds…Crashes! Two big cedars down! One trunk broke off, cannot live—The second upheaved its whole root ball! Will take bulldozers to right it, try to replant—Tomorrow call if phone works—

With cyclonic wind and fear of trees crashing, you are determined not to sleep, expect insomnia all night. While the stove works, here's rum in hot milk, this'll help you sleep—As if one cupful could save our whole world from cyclones, wars.

Crabbing in *January*?

Did summer's final jimmies pinch your mind?
I'm merely off to check the dock as usual.

You beached your traps, all they amass is snow.
Crabbing's in my genes.

Winter, crabs entomb themselves in sludge beneath the bay.
I can't hibernate, gotta look— One never knows—

Take care! The pier is slick with white!
Snow, not guano. No wind today, sun's almost warm.

No pollen now, water is transparent. You'll see no crabs down there.
I might spot one, and anyway, the coast is also clear.

Your crabs were too much work.
I did the work, I caught and cleaned. You ate.

Too cold out here…Bay's over-crabbed. And crabs give you cramps.
So we'll stash my useless traps beyond the bashed canoe
bought when the need arose to paddle mine.

*Last night's storm broke pines in two, split ends form an X beside
the silent traps: crossed boughs like scimitars bar the path. Branch
gashed your shin—*
Path striped and dotted red—You like my abstract painting in the
snow?

For God's sake, and for mine, no thanks!
You answer every question with a negative, see dark sides
of any situation or hypothesis, fish up philosophic arguments
creepy as those objects which, or who, get snagged….

Everything is seasonal. Bay frozen at these edges, now more snow—
We are all out-of-season. Sparkling, icy, treacherous, the bay waits.
I grip my crab-net pole as if a lance, check beneath the waves.

This Sunday Morning, Proust's Madeleine

"Married Sex Gets Better in the Golden Years"

New York Times, February 24, 2015

Fud-ge Swirl gelato in our second cup…
And I am swirled back more than one decade
to other Sunday mornings late in bed,
The New York Times and coffee with ice cream
till this dissolved in heat, and we in bliss.

You're eighty-three, burn brilliant, far from dead,
ichiban catbird …Memories don't fade.
Not quite so old, my every nerve tuned up
glows incandescent with ignited dreams
though Sundays now don't even rate a kiss.

One November Third: Sex Lives

"November stands on the threshold"

Aleksandr Pushkin

"My sex life: I suppose that's—"
my father lowered his voice
so I'd not hear but did, *"over?"*

Dr. Mishtowt, his old friend who'd stopped
by the nursing home, was doubtless not
surprised by the question, knew

a scant four score years old,
my father had lived a full life.
"Sorry," said the doctor, "I fear yes…"

Despite pretty nurses who'd flirt (safe from
dirty old men), my father disliked the Home,
improved and got out, I hope reversing the verdict.

So desire hangs around like autumnal hordes
of black flies and black thoughts
in the poem by Alexei Apukhtin…

Yet one persistent loud-mouthed wren
not flown south, wings in through my open door—
might build a nest here—

Au Chateau de Chillon

Instructions to Travelers

When you take the boat across Lac Léman
and reach the chateau, look around: do swans
swim toward you, stretch their long necks, hiss
for hand-outs of bread? Retrieve your fingers...

Has ivy conquered the lofty stone walls?
In the dungeons, do ghosts clank armor still?
In courtyards do hives hoard honey, bees sting?
Swallows build nests under conical roofs?

See if, under the ramparts, on the brief beach,
the handsome med student from St. Louis, MO
still waits to wed me when he graduates,

and stayed faithful since June nineteen-fifty...

Two Herpetologists Canoe the Forgotten River

At the airport, lightning flashed. Each knew who
the other must be, also knew about love on the fly.

Instead of arriving where we were meant,
we fled to the river waiting as if by design.

A green canoe lay beneath dogwood, white.
We launched her down the slippery bank,

cast off, paddled upstream, drifted in beavered ponds.
Only turtles–painted, snapper, mud and box–observed.

Our own silence was frightening, cried louder than all
the hawk calls, tree-toad chirps, frog bellows, thunder.

Alligators of longing surfaced from slow-moving murk
of the river, of our lives…Craft tippy, riverbank slippery,

was it well when true lightning flashed, slate clouds burst,
rain poured, muddy we rushed to where others awaited us…

Speculations on a Forgotten Café Napkin

Between Moroccan chicken and the grapes,
how much transpires *beyond*, what stays unsaid.
Hypotheses run (followed up by "rife"
or "rifely," says lost grammars in his head).

So starts romance that may end in bed
or never get beyond the check. Could life
become adventurous or merely shape
into parched domesticities instead?

Or end up chicken bones and rotten grapes?

"You Would Read the Palms of the Dead!"

1.

"Don't pry," you said.
I'll check your hands…

For perched on the brink let us find
where pending romance might lead:

would this last? Or become more isles
on the archipelagos of our Heart Lines?

Half-Circles of Venus beneath
fingers Two and Three reveal

sensitive/sensual souls. Too much?
Yet we *might* prove a good match:

string trios, book fairs, cinemas avant-garde,
picnics on mangoes and brie in feather beds…

2.

Remember that San Francisco cameraman?
Walking past Fisherman's Wharf 4:00 a.m.,

he saw a man, throat slit, draped over the helm
of a brig. He checked the hands, bloodied lines

showed with his flash, shape of hands.
He ran home for more spools of film.

By dawn he'd shot his fill, scribbled his notes.
He noticed a phone booth, and dialed the cops.

 "You learn," he explained, "when they are dead
if what Life and Fate Lines foretold was fulfilled,

their true natures, secrets behind Lines of Fortune.
Before light and body spoil, gotta seize opportune—"

3.

Before you and I extend our risky flirtation tonight—
But you've already paid the check, fled out of sight.

Sex Ed in *Our* Rented Garden Apartment?

The part-time preacher, part-time yoga teacher, wants to bring his yogi and yogini to classes in our basement apartment but warns: this time it'll be about sexual matters. A recent tenant at lower rent (so I'm inadvertently tithing), he's unsure of house rules. I am unsure if he wants me to participate as a student, sweep the floor after or first, provide Yogi tea, read aloud my erotic poems, or spend the afternoon off at museums. No need to make a decision yet, since this was a dream, but now awake I must hurry, write it down: dreams get lost, and the dreamer too—

Monarchs, Late Summer

The souls of old lovers return as migrating monarchs,
pause at my fig tree by the marsh though the final figs
are bird-pecked, bee-sucked, shriveled. Yet still sweet—

In this season here only in passage, the monarchs fly soon
South to a land always green, studded with luminous blooms,
find their forests of oyamel firs, overwinter and properly breed…

Yet while *our* weather is warm, their wings not yet torn,
they pause for the nectars in thistles, asters, milkweed, figs,
with their same greed for sweetness, even in spectral guise.

Elisavietta Ritchie

Which Old Lover Sent Me These Flowers?

Most are dead, the lovers. Yet one might maintain
accounts with credit at Flowers by Wire, FloristExpress,
or if kept up with technology, Google "floral bargains."

Not my birthday, though certain lovers, far to send presents,
used to remember…One dug up and brought all his excess
bamboo, which overran our garden, caused familial tempests.

This surprise bouquet includes the usual clusters of asters
purple, yellow and white, two carnations crimson as passion,
diminutive white baby's breath, the habitual fillers.

Between two stiff buds, one upstart tiger lily
demands their own vase: raffia-wrapped, a flask
stands alone on the kitchen sill.

Three purplish buds two inches long in miniature hair nets
burst into lavender spider chrysanthemums. Long blades
of dune grass, two ivory Alstroemeria, fill out this bouquet.

Can't identify every flower. On long peduncles, hundreds
of tiny green petals packed in receptacles size of coat buttons,
remain unfamiliar, mysterious… from desert or jungle?

Round flat gray-green leaves each size of a quarter
unlike any foliage in our hemisphere. Which lover
recalled my taste for exotic, tropic?

From what rampant garden, forbidden, far side
of more than one picket fence? Ah, a packet of Floralife…
I divide in three parts, and pour in the vases.

On Slippery Bricks

Familiar sidewalks of intricate bricks
once neatly fitted, now even more heaved
than several lifetimes ago, Geology 101's
raised and dropped fault blocks,
horsts and grabens in miniature.

How perilous, these mossy paths,
on either side grass mostly mud,
slick landscape topped with puddles…

You! Ghost of our clandestine affair—
brilliant, delicious, forever concealed
as supposed mere friendships should be—

so I don't slip you grasp my hand
as you did, whenever as if out just to walk
a sociable dog or do an important errand,
as if by chance we would meet on this street.

Oh, what'll the neighbors think, oh what!
we'd recite from *Under Milk Wood,*
become circumspect in our strides
while I absorbed your scent of briar pipe
and leathery books, our own pages glued…

We were glued to our diverging fates.
You reassured me you were not in pain.

Twenty-five years ago you died.
I was too far to tactfully not attend
your funeral as other friends did.

Who tossed our furtive communiqués
in a bin for recycling— into what?

Who bagged your effects for Goodwill?

Some stranger unafraid to wear the clothes
of the dead now wears your well-seasoned tweeds
and broken-in shoes, perhaps with sixth sense
to detect our secrets trapped inside soles and seams.

Does he meet *his* secret love on this street
where roots still up-heave mossy bricks?
Or is this by chance *you* taking my hand?

Yet, spirit long loved, it's no accident
you still lead me over uneven ground.

However risky the bricks, we go on…

When Isaiah Berlin Called upon Anna Akhmatova

1946, war-torn Leningrad

Neither would have nourished illusions. Though my old Russian lit professor
who'd sat at her feet, confided, "Akhmatova fell in love, indulged in affairs
when this was no longer decent,"

the erudite young British consul wished to explore her daring
dangerous mind even Stalin held, if in check, in respect.

Yet Leningrad nights in November drop below zero. Despite blankets heaped,
a widow's bed is lonely and cold. So we forgive Anna if, official tyranny set
to worsen, though she cherished Isaiah's mind

and attentions, she might have imagined his lean and warm body
wrapped around in companionable juxtaposition.

In *our* futures, may we cherish attention from handsome young guests
who have heard out our music, viewed our avant-garde art,
leafed our risky books.

We might have relished loving them when we were twenty but when
we were twenty, they still suckled their mother's breasts.

Yet let us believe we will live forever and enjoy sultry romances
even when these are no longer considered respectable for us
whether they be in November or June.

Disposal Matters

Storms wash skulls, skeletons, cast off bones
From upstream graves to downstream tombs

Most insects disappear quite neatly
To fertilize our plants they've eaten

Though beetle wings and carapaces
Hang around and leave their traces

Many spiders consume their recent webs
They need more protein with eight legs

José asks home delivery of his cinders
We flung Aunt Eugenia's in the river

All her uprooted life forever roving
Rest in Peace meant further moving

Don't leave me to my doctor daughter
Med students will dissect with laughter

How many lobsters, oysters, fishes, eels
I've hooked, scaled, cooked and peeled

Give back to the revengeful crabs
What remnants of me left to grab

I'm salty raw, stewed or frozen
Will be welcomed in the ocean

This would be the better bargain
To the end I'm green and prudent

Poet, writer, editor, translator, journalist, photographer, occasional mentor, Elisavietta Ritchie's work is widely published in the United States and abroad. Her early collection, Tightening the Circle Over Eel Country, won the Great Lakes Colleges' Association for First Books of Poetry in 1975-76, and several individual poems and stories have received awards.

Long unofficially involved with writers and poets in exile and immigration/emigration, she has translated poems from Russian, French, Malay-Indonesian, and with the help of native speakers, from other languages. Her own work has been translated into a dozen languages.The United States Information Agency sponsored her readings and meetings with local poets and writers in Brazil, Malaysia, Singapore, Indonesia, the Philippines, Thailand, Hong Kong, South Korea, Japan, the Former Yugoslavia, Bulgaria, Russia, Cote d'Ivoire and Ghana. She lived, studied and worked in France, Cyprus, Lebanon, Malaysia, Canada and Australia.

Ritchie's poems have inspired several composers, notably David Owens, Jackson Berkey, David L. Brunner and Halim El-Dabh. The chapbook Feathers, Or, Love on the Wing is a collaboration with visual artists Megan Richard and Suzanne Shelden.

She served as president of Writers' Publishing House, later as president of the fiction division.

She is a founder, with Myra Sklarew, of A Splendid Wake, an ongoing organization to honor over a century of now deceased poets who have lived and worked in the Greater Washington area. She leads creative writing workshops for adults and children. Previously a free-lance writer and photographer for the New York Times and Christian Science Monitor, now for The Bay Weekly.

The house in Washington DC, shared with her husband, journalist, writer and amateur violinist Clyde H. Farnsworth, is a frequent gathering place for writers and musicians, and a second home for numerous young scholars of many nationalities. Ritchie and Farnsworth as often live in an isolated old farm house beside the Patuxent River in Southern Maryland.

Elisavietta Ritchie

ISBN: 978-0-9909257-2-9